Rocks and Soils

John Stringer

Rocks and Soils 1

Rocks are all around you. There are rocks beneath you, wherever you are. There are rocks at the bottom of the sea.

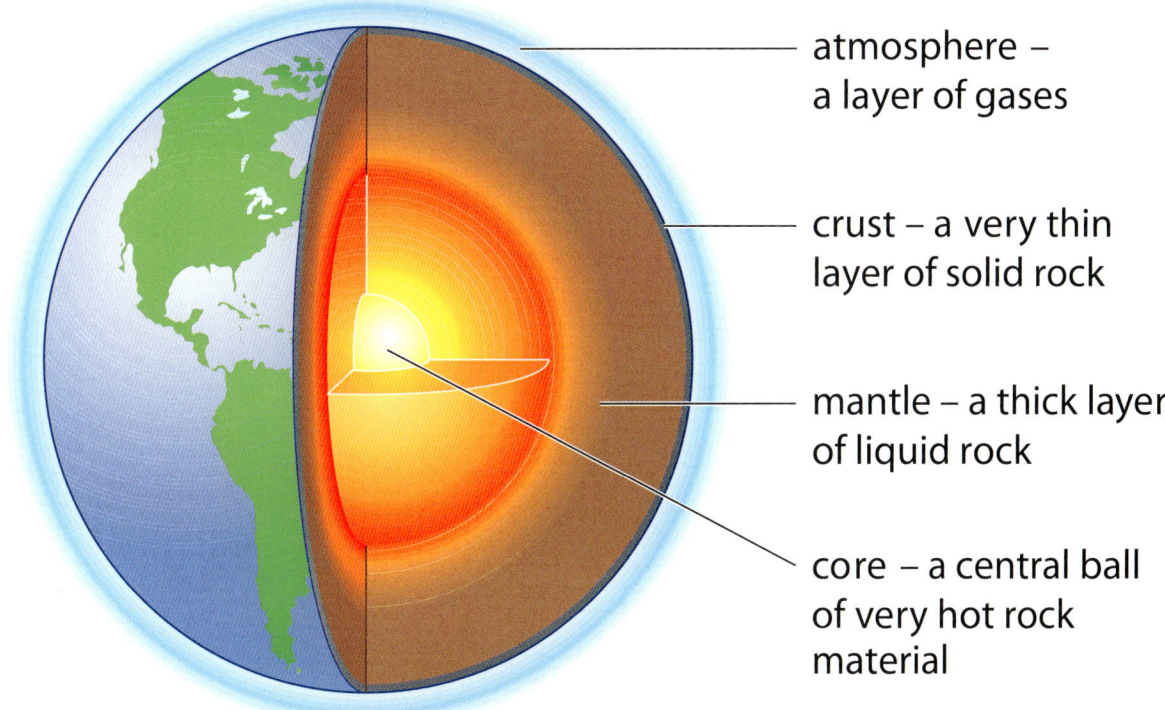

Earth is a rocky planet. But only the outer shell is hard. We call this hard shell Earth's **crust**. The inside is hot and liquid. This is Earth's **mantle** and **core**.

The Earth is like a soft-boiled egg. It has a hard shell and a hot, soft inside.

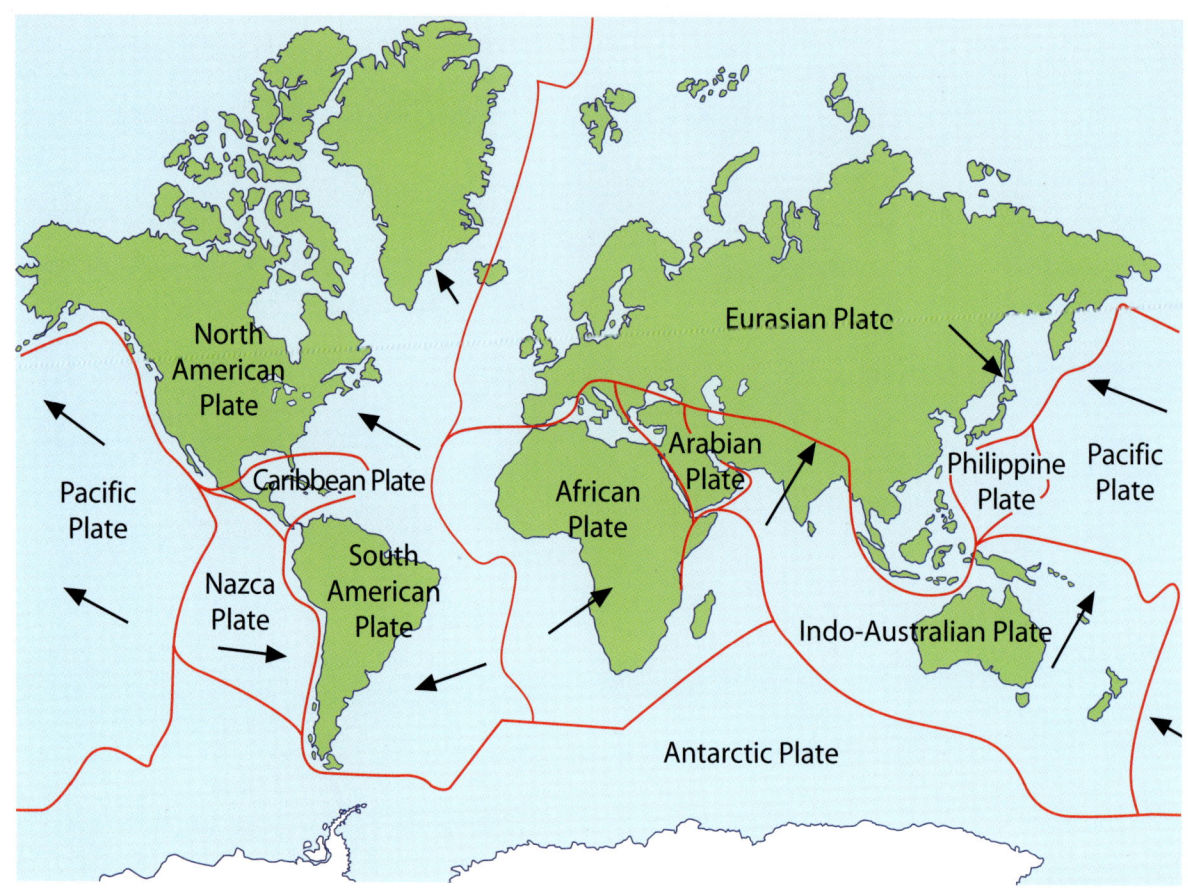

The rocks on the Earth's surface are moving very slowly. The **continents** are drifting. They move at the speed that your fingernails grow.

Once, all the dry land on Earth made one huge island. Now, it is divided into continents. They are slowly moving together again.

There are many different types of rock. Some are hard and strong. Some are soft and weak.

Some rocks are useful. We call them **minerals**. Many minerals are **crystals**. They are regular shapes with flat sides.

Some minerals are rare and beautiful. We use them to make expensive jewellery.

Diamonds and sapphires are precious minerals. Diamonds are clear, very hard, valuable stones. Sapphires are blue. We cut and polish them to show their colour and beauty.

Oil and coal are types of mineral. They are made of the bodies of living things from long ago. We can burn them as **fuel**.

Oil can be made into plastic and other useful materials.

Malachite is an ore of copper.

Some minerals are called **ores**. We mine ores. We dig for them because they can be made into metals.

Iron and **aluminium** are made from ores. At high temperatures, liquid metal pours from iron ore.

Gold has no ore. You can find pure gold in some rare rocks.

Glass is made from sand. The sand **melts** at a high temperature. The sand grains become transparent and you can see through them.

Glass is very hard, but breaks easily.

Your bathroom is full of rocks. The floor tiles may be rock. The bath and basin are made from clay. Even the mirror and windows are made from rocks.

Diamond is the hardest mineral of all. It can **scratch** every other rock. Diamond can cut glass.

Talc is the softest mineral. You can dust yourself with talc after your bath.

Cement is made by burning chalk and clay together. When the dry powder is mixed with water and sand, it makes concrete.

Concrete can be poured into **moulds** to make paving stones or bricks. When concrete sets, it hardens and becomes solid.

Sand is made of tiny grains of rock. The grains have been worn down from big rocks. It can be poured, like salt or sugar. It does not dissolve in water.

Fine sand will blow around.

Soil is made up of tiny grains of rock. Bigger grains make sandy soil. Very small grains mix with water to become clay.

Rotting plants and animals mix with the sand and clay.

There are different kinds of soil. Water **drains** quickly through sandy soils. Clay soils hold the water.

Loam is a soil with a good mixture of sand and clay. Most plants grow well in loam.

Activity

If this is the answer, what's the question

Here are the answers to some questions. Write questions that will give you these answers. If you find these answers in the book, that will help you to make the questions.

Example: The Earth's crust. You write: *What is the outer shell of Earth called?*

1. Salt and sugar.
2. The rocks on the Earth's surface.
3. Into continents.
4. Minerals are regular shapes with flat sides.
5. To make expensive jewellery.
6. Bodies of living things from long ago.
7. Gold.
8. Your bathroom is.
9. Diamond is.
10. By burning chalk and clay together.
11. Sand is.
12. Very small grains of rock.

Glossary

aluminium: a light silver metal
continent: a large area of land
core: the central part of the Earth
crust: the tough outer layer
crystal: a regular shaped mineral with flat sides
drain: to allow water to flow away from something so that it becomes less wet
fuel: a substance, such as coal, gas or oil, which burns to produce heat or power
iron: a heavy, strong metal that is used to make steel
mantle: the part of the Earth that is around the core
melt: to change from a solid to a liquid
mineral: a useful rock
mould: a container with a shape that you pour liquid into; when the liquid becomes solid, it will have that shape
ore: a mineral that is a source of a metal
rock: material from the Earth's surface
rotting: if material is rotting, it is going bad
scratch: to make a cut or mark on something with a sharp object
soil: a mixture of sand, clay and rotting material
talc: a powder you put on your skin after washing